Francisco Pizarro

Ruth Manning

Heinemann Library
Chicago, Illinois

Designed by Wilkinson Design

Printed by Wing King Tong, in Hong Kong

05 04 03 02 01
10 9 8 7 6 5 4 3 2 1

Library of Congress Cataloging-in-Publication Data
Manning, Ruth.
  Francisco Pizarro / Ruth Manning.
    p. cm. – (Groundbreakers)
  Includes bibliographical references and index.
  Summary: The life and conquests of the Spanish explorer who joined an
expedition to the New World in 1502 and subsequently claimed for Spain parts of
Mexico, Central America, and South America including Peru.
  ISBN 1-57572-369-7 (lib. bdg.)
  1. Pizarro, Francisco, ca. 1475-1541—Juvenile literature. 2.
Peru—History—Conquest, 1522-1548—Juvenile literature. 3.
Governors—Peru—Biography—Juvenile literature. 4.
Explorers—Peru—Biography—Juvenile literature. 5.
Explorers—Spain—Biography—Juvenile literature. [1. Pizarro, Francisco, ca. 1475-
1541. 2. Explorers. 3. Peru—History—Conquest, 1522-1548.] I. Title. II. Series.

F3442.P776 F67 2000
985'.02'092—dc21
[B]   00-029564
                                                              CIP

Acknowledgments   The publisher would like to thank the following for permission to reproduce photographs: The
Granger Collection Mary Evans Picture Library, pp. 4, 28, 38; Corbis, pp. 6, 29, 36; Tony Morrison/South American
Pictures, pp. 7, 22, 33; North Wind Pictures, pp. 8, 11, 14, 17, 18, 20, 27, 39; The Granger Collection, pp. 10, 25, 35; Stock
Montage, pp. 13, 26, 37; New York Public Library, pp. 15, 21; Robert Frerck/Odyssey pp. 16, 19, 30, 32, 34; Stephan L.
Alvarez/National Geographic Image Collection, p. 23; Pedro Martinez/South American Pictures, p. 24; Noboru
Komine/Photo Researchers, p. 31; Nuestra Senora de Copacabana, Lima, Peru/The Bridgeman Art Library, p. 40.

Cover photograph: The Granger Collection

Some words are shown in bold, **like this.**
You can find out what they mean by looking in the glossary.

Contents

Who Was Francisco Pizarro?

Spanish conquistador

Francisco Pizarro was a soldier and explorer who conquered new lands for Spain. After Christopher Columbus revealed a New World to Europe, many Spaniards tried to make a fortune and a name for themselves by sailing to this western territory. They wanted Spain to control new lands and profit from their resources. They also wanted to bring the message of Christianity to the people who lived in these new lands.

Pizarro was born in 1475—seventeen years before Columbus's voyage revealed the New World to Europe. By 1502, he had sailed to Hispaniola, the island that is now Haiti and the Dominican Republic. He accompanied the newly-appointed Spanish governor to this island.

By 1510, he had signed on with an expedition that was going to Colombia. In 1513, Pizarro and Vasco Núñez de Balboa were captains of the expedition. On that trip, Balboa became the first European to see the Pacific Ocean. He claimed all the lands it touched for Spain.

De A. Theuet, Liure V. 37
FRANCOIS PISARRE.
Chapitre 52.

Francisco Pizarro is remembered today mostly as the conqueror of the Incas, but his long career included expeditions all around the Caribbean.

4

Not long before Pizarro's time, Spain was divided into many smaller kingdoms. Pizarro was born in Trujillo, in Extremadura. Many other **conquistadors** came from the same area.

Conqueror of the Incas

Then in 1523, he set off on his own expedition along the west coast of Colombia, across the equator, and into what is now Ecuador and Peru. Pizarro won the permission of the king of Spain to be in charge of the territory south of Panama. In 1531, Pizarro set sail with a single ship, 180 men, and 37 horses to conquer the vast **empire** of the **Incas**—the people who controlled this territory. He succeeded.

Now he faced new challenges. He had to govern the new land, put down **revolts** of the Incas, and try to keep peace among his followers. He founded the city of Lima in Peru, and his men explored the surrounding territory. They crossed the Andes, the mountains that form a chain along the western coast of South America, and discovered the **headwaters** of the Amazon River. In 1541, Spaniards in Lima killed Pizarro.

Soldiers of Extremadura

Francisco Pizarro was born in Trujillo, Extremadura, Castile, in what is now Spain. Many of the finest Spanish soldiers came from this province, which is a high plateau land. The Romans gave this province its name from the words *extrema et dura,* meaning "remote and harsh." Villages were made up of small cottages on streets that sloped down to the center for drainage. Castles guarded **strategic** locations on the hills. Men had the reputation of being independent and stubborn. Making a living from this hard land with its summer sun and freezing winters was tough.

The harsh climate and poor soil of Extremadura make farming difficult.

Many people in Extremadura served in the army. The noble families produced the officers, and farmers and servants from the families' estates were the soldiers. They lived off the wealth that they captured during fighting. The spirit of adventure was part of their culture.

The rivers in Extremadura flow to the west toward the Atlantic Ocean. Along these river valleys, people heard news about the larger world beyond their province. Extremadura produced two of the greatest **conquistadors**—Francisco Pizarro and Hernán Cortés, the conqueror of the **Aztecs** of Mexico.

Humble beginnings

Although Francisco's parents did not record his birth, historians believe that he was born around 1475. His father was Captain Gonzalo Pizarro, also known as "One-Eyed." His mother was Francisca González, a young girl of humble birth. They were not married. According to one story, his mother abandoned her son at the entrance of the church of Santa María. Francisco's grandparents probably raised him. His father took little care of him. Had his mother and father been married, Pizarro would have inherited from his father.

From swineherd to soldier

According to another story, Pizarro took care of pigs. He never learned to read or write and became a soldier when he was a teenager. At that time, not many children had the advantage of attending school. However, many young men became soldiers. They fought against the **Moors,** who had established a presence in Spain, in a long war that finally ended in 1492. Then the noble families fought among themselves for land. Pizarro's father was an **infantry** colonel. Like him, Pizarro may have fought in the territory that is now Italy.

This statue in Trujillo, Spain, Pizarro's birthplace, shows the pride of citizens in their famous conquistador.

Spain's Role in the World

Ferdinand and Isabella

Spain came into being in 1469. This happened when Ferdinand, the eighteen-year-old king of Sicily and heir to the Kingdom of Aragon, married Isabella, the nineteen-year-old sister of the king of Castile. They had to fight wars with the Spanish nobles and the Portuguese in order to claim their thrones. Then, after the defeat of the **Moors** in battles from 1481 to 1492, Ferdinand and Isabella had no more wars to keep their military busy. In 1493, Christopher Columbus returned from the New World to the Spanish **court** with gold ornaments and six people from the islands he had visited. He opened a new world for these Spanish soldiers and adventurers to explore.

Ferdinand and Isabella rode triumphantly into Granada after the surrender of the Moors in 1492.

Tactics in the New World

The war against the Moors trained the soldiers in tactics they used in the New World. Troops were paid in what they captured. Crops and houses were destroyed to hurt the enemy. Because Spain was a Christian nation, Christianity was a strong motive in the fight against **Islam**—and later against the gods of the Native Americans. Prisoners were sent into slavery unless they could **ransom** themselves. As ransom, the families of the prisoners had to reveal their wealth so their enemies knew where to find the riches, a strategy Pizarro later used in Peru. These tactics were common in Europe at the time.

Carving up the New World

The Spanish king and queen asked the **pope** in Rome to confirm their claim to land in the New World. He issued orders that Spain owned all lands west of a line drawn between the north and south poles 300 miles (483 kilometers) east of the Canary and Cape Verde Islands. The land east of that line, including Africa, belonged to Portugal. The Portuguese had been exploring long before Columbus, and they objected to this division. The line was then moved farther west, which gave Portugal a foothold in Brazil.

Spanish dynasties

Queen Isabella died in 1504, and her husband died in 1516. Spain's rule passed to his grandson, Charles I of Spain, who already held rule in parts of Europe and was known as Charles V, the Holy Roman Emperor. Charles reigned until 1556. Spain was a dominant power in Europe, made rich by the gold and other resources from the New World.

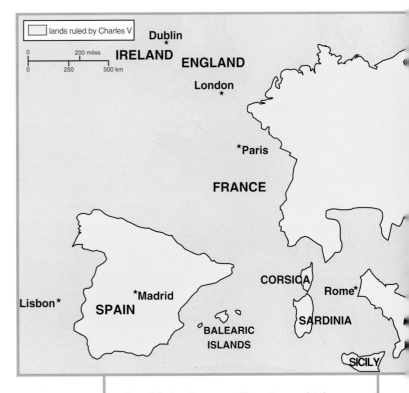

*The **Holy Roman Empire,** which Charles V controlled, included not only Spain but much of Europe. He also ruled many territories in the New World.*

FACTS

The Holy Roman Empire
This **empire** was formed long after the fall of the Roman Empire. The Holy Roman emperors would like to have controlled the territory that the Romans conquered, so they used the name "Roman" for their land. The emperors also wanted to be recognized by the pope, so they added the name "Holy."

Out to the New World

First stop: Hispaniola

By 1502, Pizarro had not gained fame or wealth as a soldier in Spain or Italy, so he had nothing to lose by seeking his fortune in the New World. He joined the expedition of Nicholas de Ovando, the new governor of Hispaniola, the island that is now home to Haiti and the Dominican Republic. Ovando was from the same province in Spain as Pizarro.

YOU CAN FOLLOW PIZARRO'S VOYAGE ON THE MAP ON PAGE 42.

D.FRAN.^{co} PIZARRO.

None of the pictures of Pizarro that have survived were done during his lifetime. They were painted from descriptions of what the man looked like.

Columbus had established the first settlement on this island in 1493, and it served as the Spanish administrative center and starting point for further exploration. Hispaniola had the oldest cathedral, **monastery,** hospital, and university in the Americas. The Spanish observed rigid class divisions and established a cruel society based on slave labor. Until gold from Mexico and Peru started to pour in, this community, with its rich mines and lands, was one of Spain's main sources of wealth.

Pizarro was a tall, well-built man with piercing eyes and a black beard. He spent seven years in the settlement, and he was a respected person.

THE SHIPS.

On to Urabá in Colombia

Settled life did not suit Pizarro. He joined the expedition of Alonso de Ojeda to Urabá on the mainland of South America. Ojeda, a commander of one of Columbus's ships in 1493, had received permission to found a settlement and search for treasure in what is now northern Colombia. Ojeda discovered a good harbor and built a settlement called San Sebastian. However, the Indians were not friendly, and they showered the Spaniards with arrows that had been tipped with curare, a deadly poison made from jungle vines and snake blood. Ojeda lost seventy men in one battle. He decided to go for reinforcements and left Pizarro in charge. Ojeda promised to return in fifty days, but his ship wrecked.

Food supplies ran short, forcing Pizarro's men to eat shellfish and seaweed. Pizarro had sixty men—too many to fit on the two small ships that he had. After six months, disease, starvation, and arrows had cut down the number of men enough that the survivors could sail away. They killed their horses and salted the meat for food on their voyage back to Hispaniola. One ship sank, which forced everyone to board the remaining one. Luckily, Ojeda's partner, Martin de Enciso, soon arrived with 2 ships, 150 men, and supplies.

To Panama with Balboa

Rescue?

Martin de Enciso, Ojeda's partner, insisted on returning to Urabá to continue the settlement. However, when they arrived, they discovered that the Indians had destroyed the abandoned houses and were still there with their arrows. Even worse, Enciso had lost one of his ships on a sandbar. Another man from Extremadura, Vasco Núñez de Balboa, took control from Enciso and sailed with Pizarro across the Gulf of Urabá to Darien, Panama, where the Indians were not hostile. He founded the town of Santa María de la Antigua, the first stable settlement on the American continent.

Balboa

YOU CAN FOLLOW PIZARRO'S VOYAGE ON THE MAP ON PAGE 42.

Balboa had come to Hispaniola to be a farmer. When that did not work out, he escaped his **creditors** by stowing away on Enciso's ship. Fortunately, he had been in this area before and knew about a good place for a settlement. He began to acquire gold by **barter** or war with the local Indians. He would support some Native American tribes against their enemies and share in the gold they won. Like many other Europeans, to gain information and obedience, Balboa used torture and ferocious war dogs that would tear their victims to pieces. When Enciso returned to Hispaniola, Balboa became the head of the colony in Panama and was recognized as the temporary governor by King Ferdinand.

Pizarro was one of many explorers, most of whom were Spanish, in the New World. Here you can see some of the most important expeditions of the time.

European discovery of the Pacific

The Indians told Balboa that to the south lay a great sea and a land of gold. He sent word to Spain. Spain sent an expedition of 2,000 persons to find gold, but because Balboa's enemies charged that he had seized control, a powerful noble, Pedro Arias de Avila (called Pedrarias) was put in charge. Before the forces from Spain arrived, Balboa sailed to the narrowest part of Panama. With Pizarro as a captain, 190 Spaniards, and hundreds of Indian carriers, he marched through dense jungles, rivers, and swamps. Twenty-five days later, on September 25, 1513, Balboa caught sight of the Pacific Ocean. He named it *Mar del Sur,* or South Sea, and claimed all the adjoining land for his king.

Balboa sighted the Pacific Ocean in 1513. When he sent word back to Spain about the sea and possible gold, the news put him back in favor with the king.

Distrust and death

When Balboa returned with his news, he regained the king's favor and was named governor of the South Sea and the province of Panama. However, he was still subject to the authority of Pedrarias, and the two men quarreled. Balboa gained permission to explore the South Sea and had a fleet of ships built and transported in pieces across the mountains to the shore of the Pacific. From 1517 to 1518, he explored the Gulf of San Miguel.

Pedrarias decided to get rid of Balboa, who was a rival for power. He had Balboa seized and charged with **rebellion,** high **treason,** and mistreatment of the Native American people. Pizarro was the arresting officer and was in charge of Balboa's execution by beheading in 1519.

Three for Exploration South

Retirement—or more expeditions?

After Balboa's death, Pizarro retired from fighting and served as mayor and judge of a newly founded town in Panama. He lived comfortably on land he had been awarded and controlled the area's inhabitants. He was in his late forties—an old man in those days. However, news of other Spaniards' conquests made him want to search for gold. He also wanted to gain a name for himself through conquests in the south.

YOU CAN FOLLOW PIZARRO'S VOYAGE ON THE MAP ON PAGE 43.

This picture shows how an artist thought Almagro—a man who was said to have been a loud-mouth with a quick temper—might have looked.

Diego de Almagro and Father Hernando de Luque

Pizarro needed help with his challenge. He turned to his neighbor, Diego de Almagro, who was in his fifties and also born of unmarried parents and unable to read or write. However, while Pizarro was tall and soft-spoken, Almagro was short, with a quick temper and a loud mouth. The two men worked together, but later they quarreled. Father Hernando de Luque was an educated man and a friend of the governor, Pedrarias, from whom the partners needed permission to sail. Pizarro discovered and explored while Almagro remained in Panama gathering and delivering supplies and reinforcements. Father Luque raised money and secured official approvals.

In November of 1524, Pizarro set sail in one of Balboa's old ships for the first of two exploration journeys. He had with him 112 Spaniards and several Indians who were trained as **interpreters.**

14

First expedition (1524–1525)

Pizarro, who had sailed with Balboa, headed south. He went up the Biru River looking for an overland route to the **empire** with the gold, but he and his men nearly starved before his supply ship returned with more provisions. They made contact with Native Americans who wore gold ornaments and who told of a powerful kingdom in the south.

With this news, Pizarro pushed farther south and found crude gold ornaments in some abandoned Indian villages. However, when his forces tried to make contact with the people from one of these villages at Quemado, they encountered a savage attack. Pizarro received seven minor wounds, and he turned back to Panama. Almagro, sailing in a second ship, also encountered fighting at this same village, and he lost an eye from a javelin wound.

The three partners brought different skills to their expeditions, but their negotiations were not always peaceful.

Request for a second expedition

Pizarro sent his **treasurer** to the governor with gold and a request for another expedition with more men. But Almagro also went to Pedrarias with a larger amount of gold. Father Luque negotiated a solution. The governor made Almagro and Pizarro joint leaders of the expedition. This shared leadership caused conflict between the two men. A contract was prepared. It stated that the conquest was in the name of God and that any people, land, and treasures would be divided equally among the three partners. Witnesses signed on behalf of Pizarro and Almagro, neither of whom could read or write.

FACTS

Gold and the Spanish

The Spaniards needed gold to fight wars in Europe. They did not care about the artistic value and melted down most items made of gold. It was quantity that won favor from the king. At first, Pizarro found only small amounts of gold, but he kept looking for the riches that the Native Americans talked about.

The Line in the Sand

The second expedition (1526–1528)

On the second expedition, 2 ships, 160 men, and a few horses were all that the two leaders could find in Panama for their expedition. Bartholomew Ruiz was important to the expedition. He was a skilled **navigator** whose seamanship helped the explorers reach Peru. He landed Pizarro in a more populated region, where Pizarro attacked and was able to capture gold and several Indians. While Almagro returned to Panama in one ship to show the gold and get reinforcements, Ruiz sailed farther south to scout the territory beyond. Pizarro and his men remained on land to discover the source of the gold.

Three months in the jungle struggling with disease, wild animals, and arrows left Pizarro's force near starvation. Ruiz crossed the equator and met an Indian trader on a **balsa** ship who had fine gold, silver, and emerald objects and news of a great source of gold in a city in the mountains.

YOU CAN FOLLOW PIZARRO'S VOYAGE ON THE MAP ON PAGE 43.

Hostile territory

With this news, the men pushed on to Atacames, a large port on the edge of the **Inca Empire.** Pizarro and his men went ashore to try to communicate with the inhabitants, but warriors surrounded them. The Spaniards escaped only because the Indians were surprised when someone was thrown from his horse. They had never seen horses before and assumed that a rider and horse were one animal. The Spaniards made a quick return to their ships.

Many people in Peru still use simple, handmade boats to travel the lakes and rivers. This raft is made from tortora reeds.

Return for reinforcements

Pizarro and his men were left on an island while Almagro returned for more reinforcements. The governor sent ships ordering the men to return to Panama. But Almagro and Father Luque sent Pizarro a letter, urging him to continue. What was Pizarro to do? His men were hungry, clothed in rags, and suffering from the harsh elements of sun and rain.

Pizarro drew a line in the sand and challenged his followers to continue with him.

Crossing the line in the sand

Pizarro is reported to have drawn a line in the sand with the point of his sword and to have said, "Gentlemen, this line represents toil, hunger, thirst, weariness, sickness, and all the **vicissitudes** that our undertaking will involve, until the day our souls will return to God. . . . There lies Peru with its riches; here Panama and its poverty. Choose, each man, what best becomes a brave Castilian. For my part, I go south." With that, Pizarro stepped over the line, and thirteen men followed him.

The ships carried the rest of the men back to Panama. Almagro, Father Luque, and Ruiz convinced the governor to send a ship for the survivors with permission to explore if they returned in six months. Pizarro ignored the limit. It was eighteen—not six—months before his ship returned with gold and news of the great empire along the coast of Peru.

Surprises

The Spaniards were amazed at the gold ornaments, the new food including sweet potatoes and maize, the llamas they called "Peruvian sheep," and the balsa rafts in this new territory. The Spaniards' beards fascinated the Indians, who had no facial hair. They tried to wash the skin of one of the dark-skinned soldiers. They thought guns, "thunder-sticks," were the homes of spirits who could cause death.

Back to Spain

Welcomed but not supported in Panama

Pizarro had been given up for dead when he returned a year later than had been planned. He was honored and entertained. However, the governor had no interest in providing the money or the men needed for conquest of the new territory. Father Luque proposed that the men make a direct appeal to the king in Spain. He could not go himself because of church duties. Because Almagro had only one eye, the men were afraid he would not make a good impression on the king. Pizarro was the only one who had witnessed the land of Peru. With his discoveries, Pizarro appeared to have gained new confidence. Pizarro assured both Father Luque and Almagro that he would look after their interests.

At the court of Charles

King Charles liked Pizarro's news of discovery. Pizarro's request for money and men to proceed with the conquest was referred to the **Council of the Indies,** a government agency that slowed down the request for a year while Pizarro's money ran out. Charles was away from Spain, so Pizarro had to **petition** the queen for the official document authorizing the conquest. On July 26, 1526, the queen signed the needed document.

Explorers had to obtain approval and support for their missions from their rulers. Pizarro and Charles V had a good relationship.

Terms of the king's agreement

Pizarro was made governor, captain-general, with a sum of money to cover an occupation force. He became a knight of the **Order of Santiago** with the right to have a **coat of arms.** Almagro was made the governor of Tumbes, a coastal city. He was only given the rank of a minor noble, with less than half the amount of money Pizarro received. Father Luque was made bishop of Tumbes and protector of the Peruvian Indians. Ruiz and the thirteen men who had crossed the line with Pizarro were given important titles but no money. In return, Pizarro was to equip a force of 250 men, 100 of whom were to come from the colonies in the New World. The Spanish government gave a little start-up money and some military supplies. The agreement also stated that the Indians were to be treated well, and that priests and **monks** would look after them to oversee their conversion to Christianity.

The Pizarro family coat of arms is carved on the wall of their palace in Trujillo, Spain.

Hometown boy returns to Trujillo

How satisfying it must have been for Pizarro to return as a hero to his old home. He persuaded four of his relatives to join him: a half-brother named Martín de Alcántara and his three brothers Gonzalo, Juan, and Hernando Pizarro. These men would have an important role in the coming conquest. At last, Pizarro had three ships but only about one hundred men. Pizarro left on one of the ships before the Council of the Indies could check it. Hernando, who remained with the other two ships, would explain that the missing number of men were on the first ship with Pizarro.

Preparations for Conquest

Facing old partners

Pizarro left Spain in January 1530, and by the next January he had departed from Panama for the conquest of new land. First, he faced the unpleasant task of telling his old partners Almagro and Father Luque what terms he had been able to secure for them from the king. Almagro was furious at the lesser position Pizarro had bargained for him. The presence of Pizarro's brothers did not help, especially Hernando's sneering attitude.

Again, the partners needed Father Luque's peacemaking abilities. Pizarro finally agreed not to give any titles to his brothers until the two partners were satisfied. **Loot** would be shared equally among the three partners. Pizarro would ask the king to give Almagro a separate territory when the conquest was complete. In January 1531, he departed from Panama for the conquest of new land.

Recruiting in the colonies

The partners did not have much success in getting men in the colonies to join their forces. Too many had seen the condition of the men who returned from Pizarro's expeditions. Some of Pizarro's former men and some of the poor settlers from Nicaragua joined. But there were still too few. Pizarro's total forces—from Spain and the colonies—was only about 180 men.

SOLDIER OF 1585.

A sixteenth-century Spanish soldier takes aim.

Armament

The soldiers had the best equipment of the day. The steel-plated armor of the men mounted on horses weighed 60 pounds (27 kilograms), but the weight was well distributed. Flexibility was built into the design. The **infantry** may have used shirts of chain mail made up of steel rings that could turn aside spears tipped with stone or copper.

The Spaniards' weapons included the harquebus gun—similar to a musket—and **crossbows.** Most battles were won in fighting at close quarters. The Spanish daggers and swords were made of **Toledo** steel, which was known for being the strongest and most flexible.

However, horses were the Spaniards' secret weapon. They used them like tanks—as both an offensive and defensive weapon. The speed of the animals made swift attack possible. Their height gave the rider an advantage in downward strokes with the sword. Pizarro had thirty-seven horses, but the Indians had none.

The artist has shown the ceremony of blessing and the departure activity on the same day though the events happened days apart.

The send-off

On December 27, 1530, Pizarro, Almagro, and their force of 180 knelt in the cathedral of Panama City to pray for the success of their crusade. Father Luque blessed them with the sign of the cross. Their banner showed St. James as a knight in armor. The church bells rang and the people cheered. The men were leaving in the service of their God and king.

The Empire of the Incas

Size of the empire

Perhaps it was good that Pizarro's 180 men did not know that they were setting out to conquer an **empire** of about 12 million people. At that time, **Inca** territory stretched more than 200 miles (3,200 kilometers) from the northern border of modern Ecuador to the Maule River in central Chile. The land included swampy jungle, deserts, and the Andes mountains—the second-highest mountains in the world. The Inca capital was Cuzco, located in a valley in what is now Peru.

Government

The emperor was cool and distant from the people. He ruled through **officials** who could be very strict. The Incas had conquered other civilizations that had lived in the area for hundreds of years. Everyone had to pay a labor tax, either by serving in the army, working on public projects, or producing agricultural crops. Practically every person farmed and produced food and clothing. The Inca empire had **irrigation** systems, palaces, temples, and forts. A remarkable road system, used only by the government and the army, had rock tunnels and vine suspension bridges. The Incas did not have a written language. Instead, they relied on a complicated system of knotted strings to send messages.

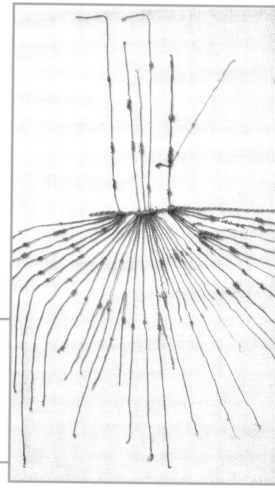

*The Incas used knotted strings, called **quipus**, to send messages. Only skilled people could interpret them. Each color or type of knot represented a different item.*

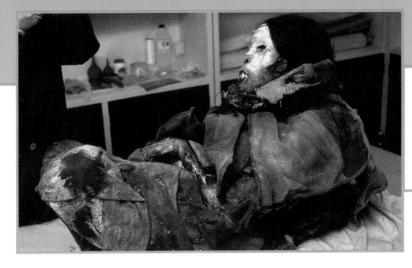

This is the body of an Inca girl that was found high in the Andes Mountains at 19,200 feet (6,000 meters).

Society

Everything belonged to the emperor, who divided land and herds. There was no middle class between the **nobles** and the common people. The common people began to work at an early age and married by age 20. An official paired off anyone who was not married by that age. Young boys who showed talent for certain skills received training. Attractive and intelligent girls were sent to a state school where they learned religion, weaving, and domestic tasks. Some of these girls became nuns of the sun god. Others became the secondary wives of the emperor or his nobles. The empress was always a full sister of the emperor. The nobles could have many wives, but commoners could have only one.

Religion

Inti, the sun god, was the chief god among other gods. Conquered people were required to worship the sun god but could keep their own gods, too. Priests **sacrificed** animals and humans to their gods. After death, the bodies of important people were **mummified** and paraded at special festival times. In recent years, the bodies of young children who were **sacrificed** on the mountain peaks of the Andes have been found in burial chambers.

Contact with the Emperor

The Incas at the time of Pizarro

Huyana Capac was the **Inca** emperor shortly before Pizarro arrived. He had heard reports of pale-skinned, bearded men in floating houses on the sea. **Prophets** had told about a people who would come from the sea to be lords of the land and who were to be obeyed. At this time, the Incas were suffering from many problems. Many lives had been lost in putting down a **rebellion.** Then a plague—possibly a European disease such as smallpox, measles, or scarlet fever—had wiped out more people, including the emperor. Before his death, the emperor had made a disastrous decision to divide his territory among his sons and to select a son named Huascar to rule after him.

The civil war

When Huascar was made the emperor in Cuzco, his brother, Atahualpa, refused to attend the ceremony. Instead, he sent gifts with messengers, some of whom were killed. The dispute escalated into a full-scale civil war. More than 100,000 of the best soldiers were killed. Huascar was captured and forced to watch as his wives and children were murdered. Atahualpa had anyone who had helped or was related to Huascar killed.

YOU CAN FOLLOW PIZARRO'S VOYAGE ON THE MAP ON PAGE 43.

EL DOZENO INGA
TOPACVCIGVAL PA
GVASCAR INGA·

In this illustration from a seventeenth-century Spanish manuscript, the Inca emperor Huascar is led away in chains by his brother's soldiers.

Because the Incas did not have horses, Inca rulers were carried into battle in **litters** by their troops.

Disappointing arrival

If Pizarro had begun his conquest a year earlier or a year later, he might have found a united Inca **Empire.** Instead, he arrived when it was at its weakest. In March, his ships were forced close to land, north of the planned landing site of Tumbes. Pizarro and some of his men went ashore to follow the land route. Although he lost the element of surprise upon his arrival, Pizarro did gain gold that he could send back to recruit more men. But his men suffered from infected ulcers, which was possibly a New World disease. And Tumbes was a disappointment because instead of the rich city Pizarro expected, he found desolation from the civil war.

Invitation from the emperor

By April, Pizarro had made contact with **officials** of the new emperor, Atahualpa. Atahualpa was living near the mountain city of Cajamarca with an army of about 30,000 men. Since he knew that Pizarro's force was small, the emperor agreed to the proposal that the two meet in the city of Cajamarca. Now Pizarro was faced with convincing his men to go into the mountains, knowing that they might be entering a trap.

By this time, Pizarro had received reinforcements of a number of horses and 100 men, commanded by Hernando de Soto. De Soto was a skilled and daring horseman who was from Pizarro's home province of Extremadura in Spain.

Battle at Cajamarca

March to the meeting

In September of 1532, Pizarro led his forces out to the meeting. He had established a Spanish settlement at San Miguel about 90 miles (145 kilometers) from Tumbes. With his reinforcements, he still had fewer than 200 men, 67 of whom were **cavalry.** About 50 soldiers were left behind to guard San Miguel, although retreat was no longer an option.

The Spaniards had to bring their troops and horses over mountain paths at high altitudes in the cold. Neither the men nor the animals were used to these conditions.

After a five-day march, Pizarro and his men rested. He offered them the chance to return to San Miguel. Nine turned back. He received conflicting reports about what Atahualpa planned and where his army was. The snow-covered mountain peaks ahead had trails that were dangerous for the men and horses. When they were not **ambushed** at an easily defended pass, they decided that the emperor did not plan an attack. The cold and thinner oxygen made their trip difficult. Seven days after they had begun their climb, Pizarro and his men could see the valley of Cajamarca and the thousands of tents of the **Inca** army.

One of the Spaniards wrote: "It filled us with amazement to behold the Indians occupying so proud a position. . . . The spectacle caused something like confusion and even fear in the stoutest bosom. But it was too late to turn back. . . ."

Forces meet

On November 15, with banners flying, Pizarro marched his army in a battle formation into a city that had been deserted on orders of Atahualpa. He sent his officers to arrange a meeting. They returned with the news that the emperor would meet the next day. Pizarro planned an ambush. He stationed his men in positions to block any retreat of the Incas and told them to keep out of sight until they heard the sound of a **musket** fire.

In the afternoon, the **sentry** warned that the Incas were on the move. Atahualpa's nobles carried him in a **litter**. But then the emperor stopped and announced that he would not enter the city until the next day. Pizarro, realizing that having to wait would discourage his men, sent word

Pizarro tricked Atahualpa into entering Cajamarca, where they met in the main square. The Incan emperor wore the red **borla**, the symbol of his rank.

that a banquet had already been prepared. Atahualpa changed his plan and entered the city with about five or six thousand of his followers.

As Pizarro had planned, the Incas were trapped in the main square. Pizarro sent out a priest, who urged Atahualpa to accept Christianity and the Spanish king. When the emperor refused, Pizarro signaled for the attack. The soldiers guarding the emperor were killed. Pizarro suffered a cut on his hand from one of the Spaniard's swords. It was the only wound in the Spanish forces. The fight had lasted a half an hour, and Atahualpa was a prisoner.

Atahualpa

After the battle

Once Atahualpa was captured, the Spaniards gave thanks for their victory. Then Pizarro entertained the emperor at the promised banquet in a hall that overlooked the square where 2,000 of the **Incas**—many of them **nobles**—lay dead. The rest of the Inca army fled. The next day, the Inca people buried their dead, the Spaniards chose the prisoners they wanted as servants, and the remaining prisoners were released. Pizarro realized that he did not have enough soldiers to move on to Cuzco immediately. He established his headquarters at Cajamarca.

Prison

Pizarro gave Atahualpa a large house and treated him with respect, although he made sure that the emperor was carefully guarded. Atahualpa was allowed to wear the clothes that showed his rank. His wives were allowed to wait on him and serve his food on gold and silver plates. He was still distant and apart from his people, but he made friends with some of the Spaniards, relaxed with them, and even learned Spanish games like dice and chess.

You can follow Pizarro's voyage on the map on page 43.

In the 1600s, a European engraver named Théodore de Bry published pictures of events like the Battle of Cajamarca. He showed the Incas without clothes on, but they actually did wear clothing.

Ransom

Atahualpa's main concern was that his brother Huascar might escape if he learned that Atahualpa was now a prisoner. He needed to free himself as quickly as possible so that his brother did not take his power. Having seen the Spaniards' love of gold, he offered to buy his freedom by filling one room with gold objects and another with silver. Pizarro agreed to this bargain. Soon the rooms were filled with objects brought from all parts of the **empire**. The emperor even ordered safe passage for the Spaniards so they could travel to some locations to make sure that the gold was being sent.

Decision for death

Pizarro agreed that the emperor had met his part of the **ransom** bargain but insisted that Atahualpa be held in **custody** for his own protection. Although several of the Spanish leaders wanted to release Atahualpa, Pizarro feared the danger of capture if he were to take the emperor with him to Cuzco. Therefore, Atahualpa was sentenced to death on charges that he had tried to cause a **revolt** against the Spaniards, had ordered his brother's death, and had more than one wife. He was to be burned at the stake, but if he would convert to Christianity and be baptized, the execution would be by strangling—an easier death. Atahualpa accepted and was killed.

About one hundred years after the capture of Atahualpa, the Spaniards built this cathedral in the Plaza de Armas in Cajamarca.

Inca Gold

Sweat of the sun

The **Incas** worshiped the sun god and considered gold to be "the sweat of the sun." About half a million pounds (220,000 kilograms) of gold were brought to Cuzco, their capital, each year and could not be removed on penalty of death. Gold was not used to buy things. Instead, beautiful objects for palaces and temples were created from gold. Plates, statues, vases, bowls—even the emperor's bathtub and its pipes—were made of gold.

The Temple of the Sun, reserved only for **nobles** and priests, dazzled with its gold. The roof was **thatch,** which kept out rain, but gold "straw" was mixed in. The walls were covered with gold on the inside and outside. A golden disk caught the morning light of the sun and provided light for the **sanctuary**, which contained a golden statue of the god. Priests wore golden robes. The temple garden had life-sized statues of gold—ears of corn, llamas, a human being, spiders, snakes, butterflies, and flowers.

You can follow Pizarro's voyage on the map on page 43.

Lost art

Few examples of Inca gold survive. Some Inca gold may have been buried. A little gold has been discovered at mountain-top burial sites. Pizarro melted down most of the gold objects he received into **ingots** that could be easily shipped. He sent some of the best gold objects to Charles V in Spain, but after putting them on display for a short time, the king had them melted down to be used as money.

Peru, the land of the Incas, was rich in gold. This drinking cup made of gold and turquoise is from around A.D. 1200.

Dividing the ransom

So what did Pizarro do with all the gold that Atahualpa had ordered brought for his **ransom**? He divided it even before the emperor had died. The Spanish king's share was one-fifth, plus some of the most beautiful objects. The rest, which would be worth millions of dollars today, was melted down into ingots and weighed in the presence of royal inspectors. Then Pizarro divided the **loot** among his men. His followers were rich.

Then Almagro arrived with reinforcements. What should be given to these men who had not shared the risk and the battle of Pizarro's men? Believing that the wealth of Cuzco still lay ahead of them, they agreed to accept less. What Pizarro did for Almagro is not known. And unfortunately, Father Luque had died before Almagro left Panama. He never knew about the success of the **venture** that he had helped create.

New uses

Charles V and his **empire** had many uses for the gold that was pouring into Spain from the New World. Some of the

This gold leaf altarpiece is in the cathedral in Seville, Spain. But many churches in Peru also had gold lavished on their art. Seville was the home port of the treasure fleets coming from the New World. The gold was used to finance wars and made Spain the richest country in Europe for three decades.

gold was used as money. But some of it was turned into magnificent things that can still be seen in the sanctuaries of churches in Spain and Peru.

Conquest and Cuzco

Consequences of the emperor's death

Following the death of Atahualpa, Spaniards could no longer travel safely in Peru. **Porters** who brought gold for the **ransom** stopped and hid their gold. Pizarro, realizing the problem immediately, chose one of the emperor's brothers to be the new leader of the **Incas.** He knew that the Incas would be easier to control if their orders came from their own emperor. Now that Almagro had arrived with reinforcements, it was time to push on to Cuzco, the capital. Pizarro marched with about 500 soldiers.

Opposition and hostilities

On the way, Pizarro found burned villages and bridges. Roving bands of troops from the civil war were still present. At Jauja, vast numbers of Inca soldiers waiting to do battle confronted Pizarro. The Spanish **cavalry** charged, and the Inca fighters fell back.

You can follow Pizarro's voyage on the map on page 43.

A scouting party led by de Soto was attacked in the Andes Mountains by thousands of Inca soldiers. The Incas did not fight at night, so when Spanish reinforcements arrived the next day, the opposing Inca force had melted away.

Inca leadership

The emperor chosen by Pizarro died. The Spaniards suspected that he had been murdered. A younger brother named Manco claimed the throne and Pizarro supported him.

The ancient Inca capital of Cuzco was designed in the shape of a puma, an animal holy to the Incas. The fort and temple complex, known as Sacsahuaman, was on the hill that formed the head of the animal. The royal palaces and other government buildings were located around a large plaza at the midsection. The homes of the noble families were in the tail, where two river canals join together.

The great Inca fortress of Sacsahuaman was built in the shape of a puma's teeth. Most of the stones were later taken for the rebuilding of Cuzco. Only about twenty percent of the original structure remains.

Triumphal entry

Thousands of Incas lined the streets of Cuzco to watch the arrival of the Spaniards with the new Incan emperor, Manco. The Incas accepted Manco but Pizarro, rather than the sun god priest, gave Manco the **borla** that was the symbol of his rank. A Spaniard then read a statement that Manco held office under the Emperor Charles. The Incas pledged loyalty to the European emperor and his governor Pizarro. A great celebration followed.

More gold

Pizarro's forces camped in the city square and were under orders not to **loot,** but the orders were often ignored. Once more, gold was collected, melted down, and distributed among the soldiers. This time, the shares were smaller because there now were nearly 500 men to reward. A few of the soldiers who returned to Spain did live well. However, most soldiers either gambled away their riches or found that they had to pay high prices for European goods.

Inca Revolt and Empire's End

Manco's revenge

The new emperor waited until the Spanish leaders, including Francisco Pizarro, had gone to other parts of Peru. Then he tried to escape. Some Indians hostile to the **Incas** betrayed him, and he was easily caught. Then Manco tricked the Spaniards by promising to get them a statue of gold. Since he was guarded by only two soldiers, he was able to break free to lead the Inca armies.

With their emperor in command, the Inca armies had new hope. They killed some of the Spaniards and their horses. Now they surrounded Cuzco and hurled burning missiles into the city to burn it down. From February to August, 1536, two hundred Spanish soldiers and about a thousand Indians hostile to the Incas held out against the Inca forces.

YOU CAN FOLLOW PIZARRO'S VOYAGE ON THE MAP ON PAGE 43.

Counterattacks by the Spanish

The Incas held the fortress of Sacsahuaman outside the city. Hernando and Juan—Pizarro's brothers—led attacks against the Incas. Juan was wounded and died shortly thereafter. Hernando captured the fortress. Meanwhile, in Lima, Pizarro was also attacked and fought back the Inca fighters.

The audience at this modern Inti Raimi Pageant shows the size of the blocks of stone that the Incas used in constructing buildings and forts.

The buildings of Machu Picchu, an Inca city east of the main mountain chain of the Andes, may have been a hiding place for Incas fleeing the Spaniards.

Capture of the last emperor

Hernando wanted to recapture the emperor. Manco's Inca fighters were not used to being away from their farms and homes for such long periods of time. By August, the emperor had been forced to let them return to plant crops for the next year. Hernando attempted to get Manco, but this time the Inca guards were effective, and he failed.

This escape was the last big victory for Manco. Still in **revolt,** he moved from one hidden fortress to another to stay ahead of the Spaniards. He carried on **guerilla** fighting for eight years until he was captured and put to death in 1544.

The end of the Inca empire

Before the Spaniards arrived, the Incas had a highly developed society. Machu Picchu, a town high in the Andes that the Spaniards never found, has provided historians with much evidence of life in the Inca **empire**.

However, the empire that the Spaniards found had already been weakened by civil war. Further fighting among themselves, attacks by the **conquistadors,** and European diseases meant the end of the Inca civilization. There are still descendants of the Incas living in Peru and nearby countries, but the once-mighty empire is gone forever.

FACTS

The Andes
The Andes are the world's second highest mountain range, measured by average elevation, with many peaks above 20,000 feet (6, 096 meters). But the Incas did not let the height stop them. Machu Picchu is built on a small plain between two peaks, at a height of 7,710 feet (2, 350 meters). The Incas built at still higher elevations in the Andes. Their capital, Cuzco, is at 11,152 feet (3,339 meters).

Spanish Conflicts

The lure of riches

Inca revolt wasn't Pizarro's only problem. Pedro de Alvarado was a **conquistador** in Mexico who held the position of governor of Guatemala. He tried to move into the northern part of Pizarro's territory and take Quito, in what is now Ecuador. However, he had followed a northern path through the cold and ice of the Andes and was easily persuaded to give up rather than meet the forces against him.

Problems with Almagro

Pizarro had sent his brother, Hernando, to Spain with gold to recruit support. Hernando brought back one of the finest armies to sail to the New World, as well as honors for those who had fought. Pizarro's territory was extended 200 miles (322 kilometers) south, and he was made a **marquis,** which is a **noble** title. Almagro was given an independent command over land 600 miles (965 kilometers) south of the Peru boundary. He claimed that Cuzco was in his territory. Because there were no accurate maps of South America, Pizarro convinced Almagro to wait for the king to make a decision and to lead an expedition south into Chile.

A dress sword with a velvet grip and decoration on the hilt was a luxury that Pizarro could afford only after the conquest.

FRANCISCO PISARRO

Almagro on the attack

Disappointed with the lack of gold in Chile, Almagro returned and captured Cuzco. He took Hernando and Gonzalo Pizarro prisoner. Civil war could not be avoided. Almagro's assistant was Rodrigo de Orgóñez, who advised his chief to kill his captives. Almagro captured the relief army that Pizarro had sent.

When Almagro and Pizarro fought over Cuzco, both men were in their seventies.

Pizarro felt that he needed first to protect his base at Lima, so he sent word to his old partner that he hoped for a friendly settlement of their dispute. Almagro refused. He prepared to leave Cuzco and move into Pizarro's territory. Gonzalo was left in Cuzco, while Almagro forced Hernando to accompany him to the coast. Gonzalo managed to escape. Pizarro offered to let Almagro keep Cuzco until the king decided whose it was. Pizarro also promised to ask his brother, Hernando, to leave Peru if he were freed. As soon as Hernando was released, Pizarro took back his offer. Hernando and Gonzalo led the attack against Almagro, who withdrew to Cuzco. After a two-hour battle, the Pizarros won Cuzco.

Almagro was found guilty of **treason** and was executed. Almagro's eighteen-year-old son, Diego, received his land.

The End of the Pizarros

Victory celebration

Francisco Pizarro came to Cuzco in 1539 to reward his men for their service and to strip Almagro's forces of land and gold. He even claimed the territory of Almagro's son Diego, which was to be ruled by Pedro de Alvarado until the young man came of age.

Hernando's sentence

Hernando then sailed for Spain to clear his name of charges brought against him for killing Almagro. But Alvarado had left before Hernando. He was a man who had great influence with the king. He told his version of the events in Peru. Even though Hernando brought a large amount of gold and silver to win the favor of the king, he was imprisoned for acts of **tyranny** in Peru. He stayed in prison for more than twenty years. Before he had left for Spain, Hernando had warned his brother, Francisco, to beware of the men who had followed Almagro.

However, Francisco let the young Diego Almagro have a large house in Lima. Francisco had made the new city of Lima his capital rather than Cuzco. It was closer to the coast and to people who sailed from Spain.

Caljou de Lima.

The Spaniards used control of the coastal areas as the key to controlling the interior of the country. Lima, with its harbor area of Callao, was an important site.

Francisco's death

King Charles was upset by the news of the fighting in Peru. He sent an **official** to find out what was happening. At first, Almagro's followers—who had been deprived of their wealth by Pizarro—waited to see the official. But when they heard a rumor that the man's ship had been lost, Almagro's followers decided to kill Pizarro while he dined with friends. Pizarro's half-brother, Martín de Alcántara, died trying to defend him. Pizarro did manage to kill three of Almagro's followers. Still, he was overpowered and killed on June 26, 1541.

Gonzalo's fate

Gonzalo had been sent off by Pizarro to explore. He reached the **headwaters** of the Amazon River. When he returned, he learned that his brother Francisco and his half brother Martín had been murdered, that the young Diego Almagro was claiming to be governor of Peru, and that the king's **official** was disputing the claim. Diego Almagro was captured and executed as a traitor. As the king's forces gained control, new laws were imposed that took away most of the wealth for which the soldiers had fought. Gonzalo sided with the soldiers and fought the royal forces. He was branded a rebel and executed in 1548.

Pizarro's followers tried to protect him from Almagro's men, but they were unsuccessful. Before he died, Pizzaro used his own blood to draw a cross on the floor.

The Pizarro brothers—except the imprisoned Hernando—and the two Almagros were dead. This was their reward from the conquest.

Pizarro's Accomplishments

Personal

So what did Pizarro accomplish? The child who had been born of unmarried parents and ignored by his father was honored by his king. Without being able to read or write, he took the gifts he had—his training as a soldier—and put them to work. Against amazing odds, he succeeded at conquering the **Inca** empire.

Discoverer

To go to the New World from Spain took courage. How much more courage was required to go into a strange territory! Pizarro found an ocean that Europeans did not know existed. He marched through jungles infested with wild animals, disease, and unfriendly natives. He discovered a land and a people, the Incas, who were unknown to Spaniards. He climbed mountains higher than any he had ever seen. He outfitted the expedition of a brother who found the **headwaters** of the great Amazon River.

Conqueror

Even though Pizarro met the Incas at their weakest, he had to face overwhelming odds in the fighting. He used strategies to achieve his goals. He has been criticized for his cruelty and failure to keep promises to others. Yet the Spanish society in which he was raised, and the Inca society that he observed, encouraged these traits. He was able to rule as governor—far

The coming of Pizarro and the Europeans completely changed life for the Incas of Peru. This eighteenth-century painting shows the wedding of two Inca women to Spaniards. While the woman on the left is wearing the clothing of her people, the other woman wears European **court** *dress.*

from his king's authority—the vast territory of Peru that was drawing many Spaniards to the New World. Should Spain have tried to conquer the Incas? The question would not have occurred to Pizarro, whose family had fought the **Moors** in Spain and Europeans in Italy.

Founder

Pizarro founded the city of Lima and established many Spanish institutions. He brought the Christian church and the Spanish language to Peru. In doing so, he destroyed much of the beauty of Inca art, as well as the government of the Inca emperor. Yet, he also was responsible for the founding of a new people, because Spaniards and Incas married.

Maps

These two maps show the routes of Pizarro's journeys. On his earlier journeys, shown in the map below, Pizzaro was in the company of other men, such as Christopher Colombus and Balboa. However, on his later journeys, shown at right, Pizarro led the expeditions that helped vanquish the Inca empire.

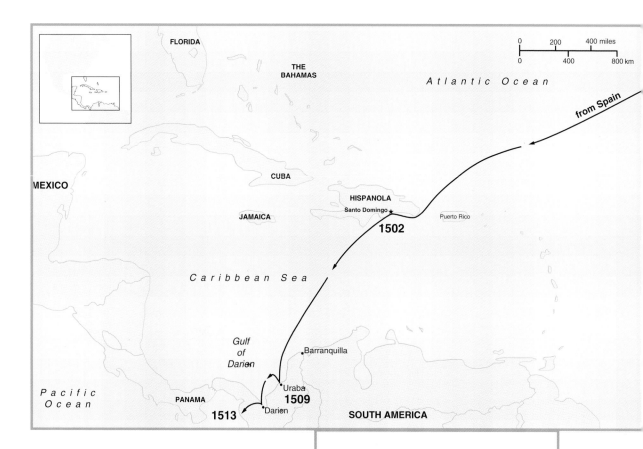

Pizarro's early explorations in the New World led him to the shore of the Pacific Ocean.

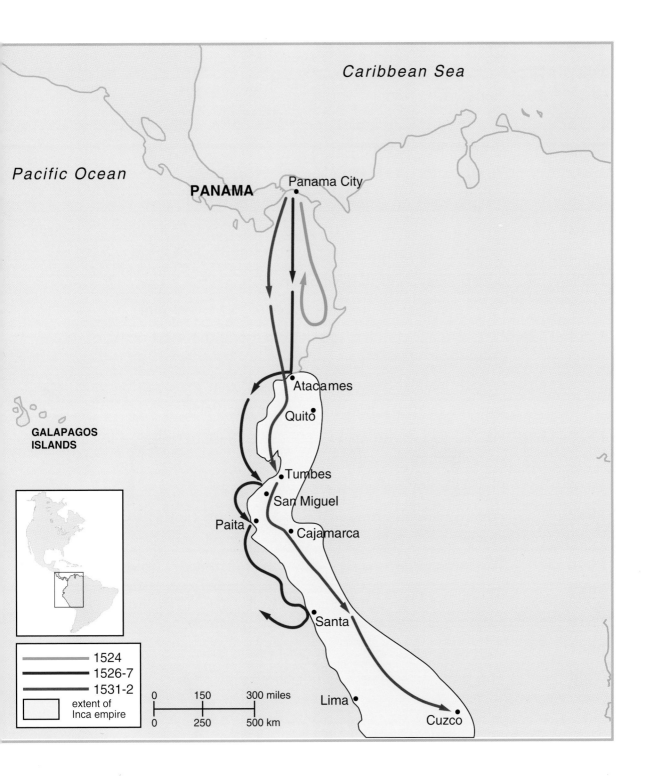

Caribbean Sea

Pacific Ocean

PANAMA   Panama City

Atacames

Quito

GALAPAGOS
ISLANDS

Tumbes

San Miguel

Paita

Cajamarca

Santa

1524
1526-7
1531-2
extent of
Inca empire

0   150   300 miles

0   250   500 km

Lima

Cuzco

Timeline

1469	Ferdinand and Isabella marry and unify two Spanish kingdoms, Aragon and Castile.
1475	Pizarro is born.
1481–1492	Ferdinand and Isabella battle against the **Moors** and drive them from Spain.
1493	Christopher Columbus returns to Spain with news of land across the Atlantic Ocean.
1502	Pizarro sails to Hispaniola.
1510	Pizarro joins an expedition to Urabá in Colombia.
1513	Pizarro is a captain with Vasco Núñez de Balboa, who is credited as the European who discovered the Pacific Ocean.
1516	Charles becomes king of Spain.
1519	Pizarro arrests Balboa with orders to behead him.
1524–1525	Pizarro leads the first expedition along the west coast of Colombia.
1526–1527	Pizarro leads the second expedition that crosses the equator and lands in territory now in Ecuador and Peru.
1528–1530	Pizarro returns to Spain to get the king's permission for an expedition of conquest.
1530	Pizarro leads the conquest of the **Incas**.
1532	Pizarro wins the Battle of Cajamarca and captures the Inca emperor.
1536	The Incas counterattack in Cuzco, but the city holds out.
1537	Almagro captures Cuzco from Pizarro's brothers.
1539	Almagro is executed for committing **treason.**
1541	Pizarro is killed by followers of Almagro.
1544	The last Inca emperor is put to death.

More Books to Read

Gonzalez, Christina. *Inca Civilization*. Danbury, Conn.: Children's Press, 1993.

Jacobs, William H. *Pizarro: Conqueror of Peru*. Danbury, Conn.: Watts, Franklin Inc., 1994.

Johnstone, Michael. *Explorers*. Cambridge, Mass.: Candlewick Press, 1997.

Lyle, Garry. *Peru*. Broomall, Penn.: Chelsea House Publishers, 1998.

Martel, Hazel. *Civilizations of Peru before 1535*. Austin, Tex.: Raintree Steck-Vaughn Publishers, 1999.

Sanchez, Richard. *Spain: Explorers and Conquerors*. Minneapolis, Minn.: ABDO Publishing Company, 1994.

Tames, Richard. *Great Explorers*. Danbury, Conn.: Watts, Franklin, Inc., 1997.

Glossary

ambush hidden place from which a surprise attack can be made; also to make a surprise attack

Aztecs Native Americans of Mexico who had a highly developed civilization at the time the Spaniards came

balsa very lightweight wood that comes from trees that grow in South America

barter to trade one thing for another, without using money

borla special fringed headdress worn by the Inca emperor

caravel small ship with three or four masts, used in the fifteenth and sixteenth centuries

cavalry soldiers mounted on horseback

coat of arms group of designs and figures that is the special sign of a person or family, and that only very rich people, nobles, or knights were allowed to have

conquistador leader in the Spanish conquest of the Americas during the fifteenth and sixteenth centuries

Council of the Indies Spanish council that made decisions about the New World

court a ruler's assembly of advisers and officers

creditor person or company to whom someone owes money

crossbow bow mounted on a wooden handle that shoots short arrows

custody in jail or in the keeping of police or soldiers

empire group of territories or people under one ruler

guerilla style of fighting in which a small group of soldiers make sneak attacks behind enemy lines, sometimes over a long period of time

headwaters beginning and upper part of a stream or river

Holy Roman Empire empire lasting from the ninth through the eighteenth centuries, consisting mostly of German and Italian states and ruled by a single emperor

Incas Native American people of Peru who had a highly developed civilization when the Spaniards came

infantry branch of an army made up of soldiers who fight on foot

ingot bar of gold that is a standard shape, weight, and size

interpreter person who can translate one language into another

irrigation system of bringing water from a river or lake to water crops

Islam religion based on belief in Allah, started by the religious leader Muhammad, whose followers are called Muslims

javelin light spear used for throwing

litter covered couch with poles, used for carrying a single passenger

loot to rob or steal openly and by force; also the things gotten by doing so

marquis noble ranked higher than an earl but below a duke

monastery place where a group of religious men live and work

monk male member of a religious community who devotes his life to work and prayer

Moors Muslims from northern Africa who conquered Spain in the eighth century

mummify to keep a dead body from rotting by treating it with chemicals

musket gun with a long barrel, used before the rifle was invented

navigator officer on a ship responsible for figuring out its position and course

official person who acts with authority of a ruler or government

Order of Santiago highest order of knighthood in Spain

petition to make a request to someone in power, such as a king or queen

pope leader of the Roman Catholic Church

porter person whose job is to carry things

prophet religious leader whom people believe speaks for a god or for God

province part of a country that has its own government

quipus knotted cords used by the Incas to send messages and remember things

ransom money paid to free a person from captivity or punishment

rebellion open fight against the government, also called a revolt

revolt open fight against the government, also called a rebellion

sacrifice to make an offering, sometimes by killing a person or animal, to a god in a special ceremony

sanctuary place for religious worship or where a person can find safety and shelter

sentry person on duty as a guard

strategic having a location or quality that is useful in warfare, such as being at the top of a hill from which the enemy's movements can be seen

thatch plant, such as straw, used for roofing

Toledo area in Spain that was known for its high-quality steel and for sword-making

treason crime of trying to overthrow the government of your own country

treasurer official who is in charge of an organization's money

tyranny cruel or unfair use of power

venture project that may be dangerous or risky

vicissitude difficulty or change caused by a situation or a way of life

Index